WELCOME!

From the tallest to the longest and from the busiest to the largest, this book looks at fantastic record-breaking buildings from all over the planet and beyond! It uses stunning icons, graphics and visualisations to show you how these structures have raised the bar in the construction industry.

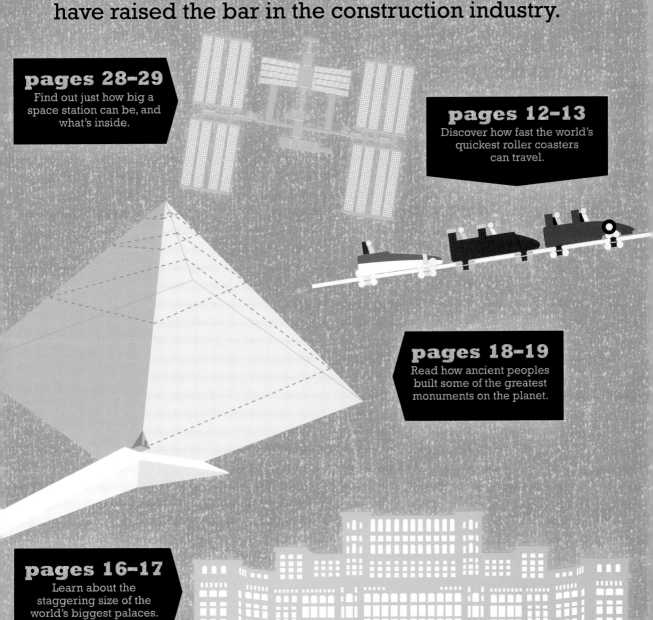

pages 28–29
Find out just how big a space station can be, and what's inside.

pages 12–13
Discover how fast the world's quickest roller coasters can travel.

pages 18–19
Read how ancient peoples built some of the greatest monuments on the planet.

pages 16–17
Learn about the staggering size of the world's biggest palaces.

TALLER AND TALLER

Advances in technology over the last 100 years have seen the world's tallest buildings nearly quadruple in size. The biggest skyscrapers are now nearly a kilometre high and really do have their heads in the clouds!

Moving Tower

Changes in temperature throughout the year cause the Eiffel Tower to expand and contract by as much as 18 cm. Powerful winds also push the top of the tower, causing it to sway by 7 cm.

7 cm

These graphics show

the buildings that have held the title of the world's tallest building over the last 100 years. They are compared to the height of a giraffe.

x 74

At just 301 m tall, the Eiffel Tower in Paris is less than half the height of the Burj Khalifa.

1

2

3

4

5

6

7

8

9

10

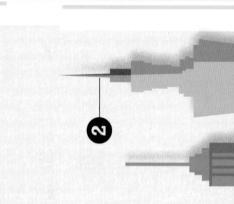

TALLEST BUILDINGS THROUGH HISTORY

1. **Burj Khalifa, Dubai (since 2010) – 828 m**

2. **Taipei 101, Taiwan (2004–2007) – 509 m**

3. **Petronas Towers, Malaysia (1998–2004) – 452 m**

4. **Willis Tower, USA (1974–1998) – 442 m**

5. **World Trade Center, USA (1972–1974) – 417 m**

6. **Empire State Building, USA (1931–1972) – 381 m**

7. **Chrysler Building, USA (1930–1931) – 319 m**

8. **The Trump Building, USA (1930) – 283 m**

9. **Woolworth Building, USA (1913–1930) – 241 m**

10. **Metropolitan Life Building, USA (1909–1913) – 213 m**

Empire State Building

This skyscraper is struck by lightning on average 23 times a year.

The observatory on the 102nd floor was originally designed to be a check-in area for airships that would moor to the top.

x 138

x 85

x 75

x 64

x 53

x 47

x 40

x 36

SPEND, SPEND, SPEND

Shopping malls are enormous buildings that can contain hundreds of shops. Many of the largest also feature theme parks, restaurants and cinemas to keep shoppers happy and spending their money.

Mega mall

The Dubai Mall is the largest mall in the world in terms of total area, but only the 14th largest in terms of leasable area (the area taken up by shops).

shops 1,200

200 restaurants

It has the world's largest sweet shop – Candylicious. This covers 930 sq m, which is about **1.5 football pitches.**

It has 80 million visitors every year...

Germany: population 80,996,000

... more than any other place on Earth and close to the total population of Germany.

Its shops can take more than £3 billion in a year...

£1,400

... that's enough to give every person living in Dubai £1,400 per year.

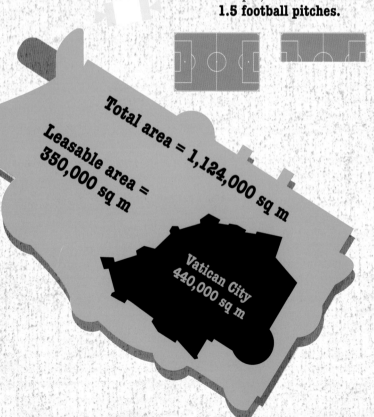

Total area = 1,124,000 sq m

Leasable area = 350,000 sq m

Vatican City 440,000 sq m

Supermarkets

The first supermarket in the US was King Kullen Supermarket, which opened on Jamaica Avenue, New York City, in August 1930.

It covered just 560 sq m (a basketball court is 420 sq m).

In contrast, Jungle Jim's International Market, in Ohio, USA, covers more than 18,500 sq m – more than 30 times the area of King Kullen Supermarket and three times the area of the White House.

Walmart is one of the biggest supermarket chains in the world.

It has...

more than 11,000 stores in **27 countries** and employs **2.2 million staff**

LARGEST SHOPPING MALLS (LEASABLE AREA)

1. **New South China Mall (Dongguan, China) – 600,153 sq m**

2. Golden Resources Mall (Beijing, China) – 557,419 sq m

3. **SM Megamall (Mandaluyong, Philippines) – 506,435 sq m**

4. SM City North EDSA (Quezon City, Philippines) – 482,878 sq m

5. **1 Utama (Petaling Jaya, Selangor, Malaysia) – 465,000 sq m**

6. Persian Gulf Complex (Shiraz, Iran) – 450,000 sq m

7. **Central World (Bangkok, Thailand) – 429,500 sq m**

8. Isfahan City Center (Isfahan, Iran) – 425,000 sq m

=9. **Mid Valley Megamall (Kuala Lumpur, Malaysia) – 420,000 sq m**

=9. Cevahir Mall (Istanbul, Turkey) – 420,000 sq m

NO X̶P̶ SPARED

Welcome to the most expensive buildings on the planet! They offer bespoke office services, amazing hotel accommodation and the height of private luxury.

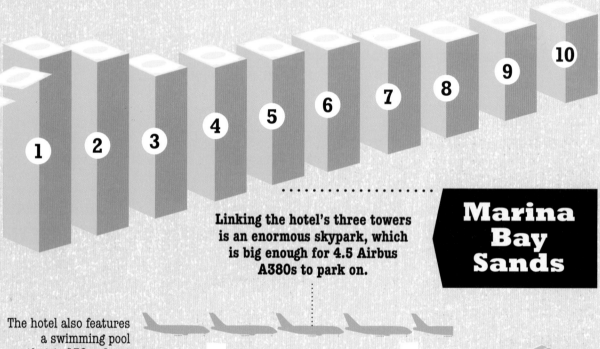

1 2 3 4 5 6 7 8 9 10

Linking the hotel's three towers is an enormous skypark, which is big enough for 4.5 Airbus A380s to park on.

Marina Bay Sands

The hotel also features a swimming pool that is **150 m long**, a shopping mall, a museum, two theatres and an ice rink.

The largest suites in the Marina Bay Sands measure 629 sq m, about the same area as **two tennis courts.**

It was built at a rate of one floor **every four days.**

The casino inside the hotel has a chandelier which contains 132,000 crystals and weighs 7.1 tonnes – about the weight of three adult hippos!

MOST EXPENSIVE BUILDINGS

1. **Marina Bay Sands (Singapore) – US$6 bn**

2. Resorts World Sentosa (Singapore) – US$5.38 bn

3. **Emirates Palace (Abu Dhabi) – US$4.46 bn**

4. The Cosmopolitan (USA) – US$4.16 bn

5. **The Shard (UK) – US$3.9 bn**

6. One World Trade Center (USA) – US$3.8 bn

7. **Wynn Resort (USA) – US$3.26 bn**

8. Venetian Macau (Macau) – US$2.97 bn

9. **City of Dreams (Macau) – US$2.75 bn**

10. Antilia (India) – US$2.53 bn

The prices of these buildings have been adjusted for inflation so that the figures here show the cost if they were all built in 2012.

Living in luxury

The Burj al Arab is a seven-star hotel in Dubai. It has nine restaurants and bars, a health spa, four swimming pools, its own private beach and a helicopter landing pad on the roof.

 x9 x4 x1 x1

A Royal Suite here can cost up to £11,435 for a single night!

Most expensive hotel suite

The Royal Penthouse Suite at the Hotel President Wilson, Geneva, Switzerland can cost up to US$83,200 a night.

It has 12 bedrooms, 12 bathrooms, a gym, a billiards table and a grand piano.

The suite covers 1,800 sq m – larger than the area of four basketball courts.

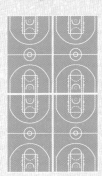

Antilia

Antilia is said to be the most expensive private residence in the world. It has **three helipads** and a multi-storey garage with space for **168 cars**.

168

...... Owned by Indian billionaire Mukesh Ambani, Antilia is located in the city of **Mumbai, India.**

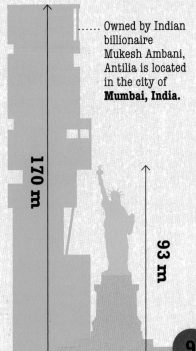
170 m
93 m

ON DISPLAY

Millions of people flock to museums around the world every year. These buildings house precious works of art, animal bones and fossils, historical relics and monuments, or amazing inventions. They also have huge storage areas where they keep objects that they cannot display.

1
2
3
4

👤 = 500,000 visitors

The Smithsonian

The Smithsonian Institution is the world's largest museum complex. It is made up of 19 galleries and museums and houses more than

137 million objects.

If you spent one minute looking at each object for 24 hours a day, it would take more than 260 years to view them all!

| 1 min x 🦏 x 24 hrs |

= 260 years

The British Museum

It has a total area of 92,000 sq m, of which 21,600 sq m is storage space (with a further 9,400 sq m of storage space offsite).

The British Museum can display about 80,000 items at any one time – but that's just 1 per cent of the 8 million items it owns.

MOST POPULAR MUSEUMS

1. **Louvre (Paris) – 9,334,000 visitors a year**
2. National Museum of Natural History (Washington, DC) – 8,000,000
3. **National Museum of China (Beijing) – 7,450,000**
4. National Air and Space Museum (Washington, DC) – 6,970,000
5. **British Museum (London) – 6,701,000**
6. The Metropolitan Museum of Art (NYC) – 6,280,000
7. **National Gallery (London) – 6,031,000**
8. Vatican Museums (Vatican) – 5,459,000
9. **Natural History Museum (London) – 5,250,000**
10. American Museum of Natural History (NYC) – 5,000,000

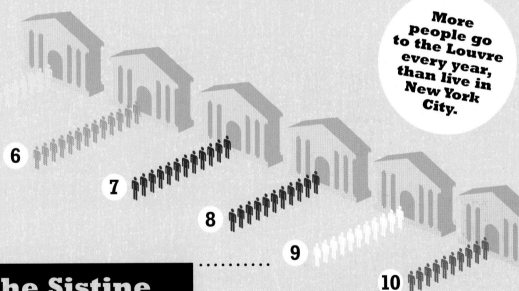

More people go to the Louvre every year, than live in New York City.

The Sistine Chapel

The Vatican in Rome houses a number of museums, including the Sistine Chapel. The ceiling of this features an enormous fresco painted by Michelangelo.

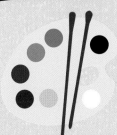

The fresco covers 800 sq m (more than three tennis courts) and took four years to paint (1508–1512).

FUN AND GAMES

Strap in, hold on and get ready to discover the adrenalin-fuelled world of the planet's top theme parks! They cater for millions of people and offer the most thrilling rides on Earth.

3 **Top Thrill Dragster**
Cedar Point, Sandusky, Ohio, USA
192 km/h

4 **Dodonpa**
Fuji-Q Highland, Yamanashi, Japan
171.2 km/h

=5 **Tower of Terror**
Dreamworld, Queensland, Australia
160 km/h

=5 **Superman: Escape from Krypton**
Six Flags Magic Mountain, Valencia, California, USA
160 km/h

Tallest roller coaster

The tallest roller coaster in the world is the Tower of Terror at Dreamworld amusement park in Queensland, Australia. It is 115.01 m tall – more than twice the height of **Nelson's Column**, London (52 m), and a little shorter than **St Peter's Basilica**, Rome (138 m).

10 **Leviathan**
Canada's Wonderland, Mapl Ontario, Canada
147.2 km/h

Formula Rossa

1

Ferrari World, Yas Island, Abu Dhabi

238.6 km/h

Kingda Ka

2

Six Flags Great Adventure,
Jackson, New Jersey, USA

204.8 km/h

Ferrari World is the largest indoor amusement park in the world. It covers a total of 200,000 sq m and the indoor area is 86,000 sq m – as big as seven American football fields.

Ferrari World

Formula Rossa at Ferrari World in Abu Dhabi is the fastest roller coaster in the world. It accelerates from **0–100 km/h in 2 seconds** – that's as fast as a Formula 1 car.

Ring racer

7

Nürburgring, Nürburg, Germany

159 km/h

Steel Dragon

8

Nagashima Spa Land,
Nagashima, Japan

152 km/h

Millennium Force

9

Cedar Point, Sandusky, Ohio, USA

148.8 km/h

In total, the 10 most popular theme parks attract 126,669,000 people every year – that's more than the total population of Mexico.

13

BUILDING FOR ANIMALS

Animals need lots of space to live in – some zoos cover enormous areas! They also need to meet each animal's specific needs and be super-tough to withstand tonnes of water and strong beasts.

Hengoin Ocean Kingdom

The aquarium at the Hengoin Ocean Kingdom holds enough water to fill nearly 20 Olympic swimming pools.

1

2

Big bird park

Located in Kuala Lumpur, Malaysia, the KL Bird Park is the largest free flight aviary in the world. It covers 8.5 hectares and is home to 3,000 birds from 200 species.

LARGEST AQUARIUMS (LITRES)

1. **Hengoin Ocean Kingdom (China) – 48.72 million**
2. Georgia Aquarium (USA) – 23.84 million
3. **Dubai Mall Aquarium (Dubai) – 9.99 million**
4. Okinawa Churaumi Aquarium (Japan) – 7.5 million
5. **L'Oceanografic (Spain) – 7 million**
6. Turkuazoo (Turkey) – 5 million
7. **Monterrey Bay Aquarium (USA) – 4.54 million**
=8. uShaka Marine World (South Africa) – < 3.8 million
=8. **Shanghai Ocean Aquarium (China) – < 3.8 million**
=8. Aquarium of Genoa (Italy) – < 3.8 million

The penguin pool at London Zoo covers 1,200 sq metres and holds 450,000 litres. That's enough to fill more than 5,500 baths and give you a bath every day for the next 15 years!

x 5,500

Penguin pool

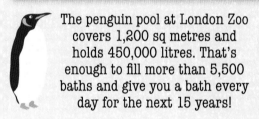

3 4 5 6 7 8 9 10

One wall of the Dubai Mall Aquarium is made from an enormous panel of transparent acrylic – the largest in the world. It measures 32.88 m by 8.3 m, making it bigger than a tennis court.

Toronto zoo

Toronto Zoo is one of the largest zoos in the world. It has over 5,000 animals from 500 different species.

The zoo has 10 km of walking trails (enough to go around an athletics track 25 times) and covers 287 hectares – about the same size as Central Park in Manhattan, New York City, USA.

- Central Park

Manhattan

FIT FOR A KING

<----------------------------------->

Royal palaces are some of the most opulent and imposing buildings on the planet. Inside, the rooms are decked out in the height of luxury.

The Hall of Mirrors at the Palace of Versailles contains **357** mirrors.

The enormous Louvre palace in Paris covers more than 1.5 times the area of the Pentagon building.

The Forbidden City

The Forbidden City in Beijing is part of a huge palace complex that covers **74 hectares** in total.

Palace of Parliament, Bucharest

It is the world's heaviest building, with **700,000 tonnes** of steel and bronze...

... that's twice the weight of the Empire State Building.

LARGEST ROYAL PALACES

1. **Louvre (Paris, France) – 210,000 sq m**
2. Istana Nurul Iman (Bandar Seri Begawan, Brunei) – 200,000 sq m
3. **Apostolic Palace (Vatican City) – 162,000 sq m**
4. Forbidden City (Beijing, China) – 150,000 sq m
5. **Royal Palace of Madrid (Madrid, Spain) – 135,000 sq m**
6. Quirinal Palace (Rome, Italy) – 110,500 sq m
7. **Buckingham Palace (London, UK) – 77,000 sq m**
8. Topkapi Palace (Istanbul, Turkey) – 70,000 sq m
9. **Palace of Versailles (Versailles, France) – 67,000 sq m**
10. Royal Palace of Stockholm (Stockholm, Sweden) – 61,120 sq m

It has 1 million cubic m of marble

– that's enough to fill

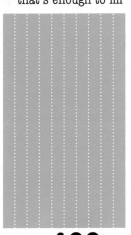

x 400
Olympic swimming pools

Inside, there are **3,500 tonnes** of glass, which is equivalent to the weight of...

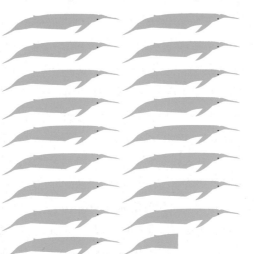

... 17.5 blue whales.

The glass is used in **1,409** lights and mirrors, and...

... **480** chandeliers.

It has 200,000 sq m of carpet
– enough to cover...

... 4 polo fields

ANCIENT BUILDINGS

The oldest surviving buildings in the world were built nearly 7,000 years ago. These ancient constructions are usually tombs, monuments or, like Stonehenge, puzzling structures whose real use remains a mystery.

Stonehenge

This ancient monument was started about **5,000 years** ago and built over a period of **1,000 years.**

Each stone weighs 22.5 tonnes...

... as much as four elephants.

How it was built

Larger stones were levered into pits until they stood upright. Smaller stones were then raised using levers and platforms, before being pushed in place on top of the upright stones.

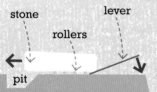

stone
rollers
lever
pit

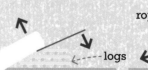

logs

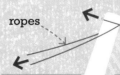

ropes

| The larger stones were moved on rollers into place by a pit. One end of the stone was then raised using a lever. | Logs were placed under the raised end to keep it in place. The lever was used again to raise the stone even higher. | Ropes were then attached to lift the stone so that it was upright, with one end in the pit. | Finally, the pit was filled in, to hold the upright stone firmly in place. |

OLDEST BUILDINGS IN THE WORLD

=1. Barnenez, France – around 4800 BCE

=1. Tumulus of Bougon, France – around 4800 BCE

=1. Tumulus Saint-Michel, France – around 4800 BCE

=4. Wayland's Smithy, UK – around 3700 BCE

=4. Knap of Howar, UK – around 3700 BCE

=4. Ggantija, Malta – around 3700 BCE

7. West Kennet Long Barrow, UK – around 3650 BCE

8. Listoghil, Ireland – around 3550 BCE

=9. Sechin Baho, Peru – around 3500 BCE

=9. La Hougue Bie, Jersey – around 3500 BCE

Great pyramids

Egypt has about **140 pyramids**, which were built as burial chambers for important people. They can be stepped, bent, or have a true, triangular shape.

These ancient buildings were constructed more than 4,500 years ago. The **Pyramid of Khufu** is the largest and it contains **2.3 million stones,** and weighs more than **5 million tonnes.**

The heavy stones were dragged by teams of workers up ramps that wrapped around the pyramid.

It was originally 147 m tall and was the tallest building in the world for more than 3,500 years.

internal ramps

ramp

True – Giza

Bent – Dahshur

Stepped – Saqqara

Pyramids of Queens

Pyramid of Menkaure

Pyramid of Khafre

Pyramid of Khufu

The pyramids of Giza

ON THE MOVE

Millions of people travel around the globe every year, flying from huge airports or boarding trains from busy stations. At the same time, enormous cargo ships carry billions of tonnes of cargo to bustling ports and freight terminals.

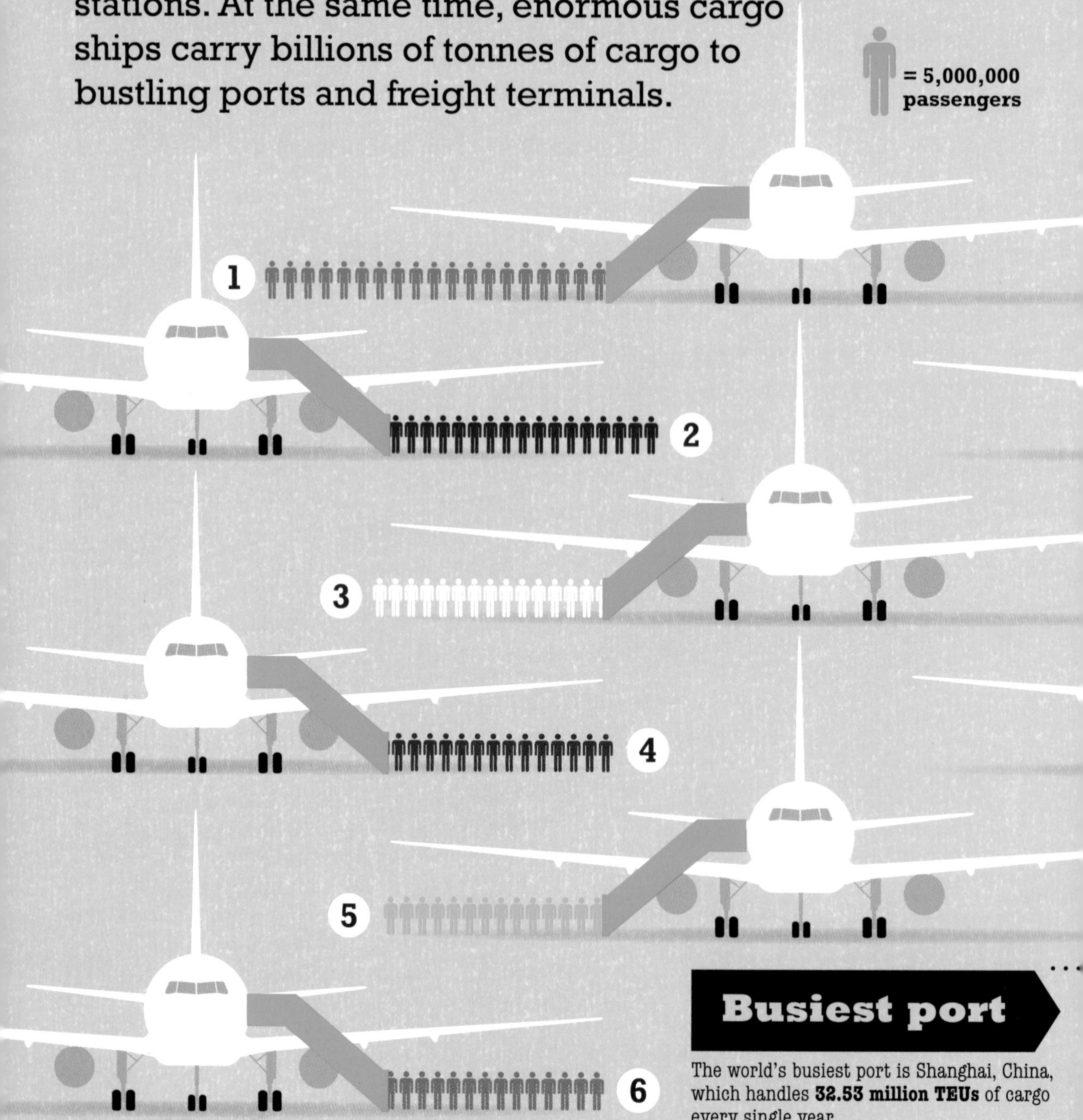

= 5,000,000 passengers

1

2

3

4

5

Busiest port

The world's busiest port is Shanghai, China, which handles **32.53 million TEUs** of cargo every single year.

6

1. **Atlanta, USA – 94,778,483 passengers per year**

2. Beijing, China – 84,187,266

3. **Heathrow, UK – 73,036,493**

4. Tokyo, Japan – 70,680,743

5. **Los Angeles, USA – 68,783,018**

6. Dubai, UAE – 68,445,520

7. **Chicago, USA – 68,329,963**

8. Paris (CDG), France – 63,311,851

9. **Dallas/Fort Worth, USA – 61,744,158**

10. Hong Kong, China – 61,485,440

About 93 per cent of the passengers travelling through Heathrow airport are using international flights. That figure for Atlanta airport is around 10 per cent.

7

8

9

10

LARGEST TRAIN STATION

Grand Central Terminal in New York City is the world's largest train station in terms of the number of platforms. It has 44 of them handling 660 trains and 125,000 commuters every single day.

TEU stands for 'twenty-foot equivalent units', which is the size of a standard shipping container. One of these holds **38.5 cubic m**, which is about...

250 full baths of water.

This means that Shanghai handles about **1.25 billion cubic m** of cargo every year, or **140,000 cubic m** every single hour (working 24 hours a day and 365 days a year!).

That's enough to fill 20 blimps.

BRIDGE IT – GATE

The world's greatest bridges are amazing feats of technology. They are capable of carrying thousands of tonnes of trucks, cars and buses over wide rivers, deep valleys and even whole stretches of ocean.

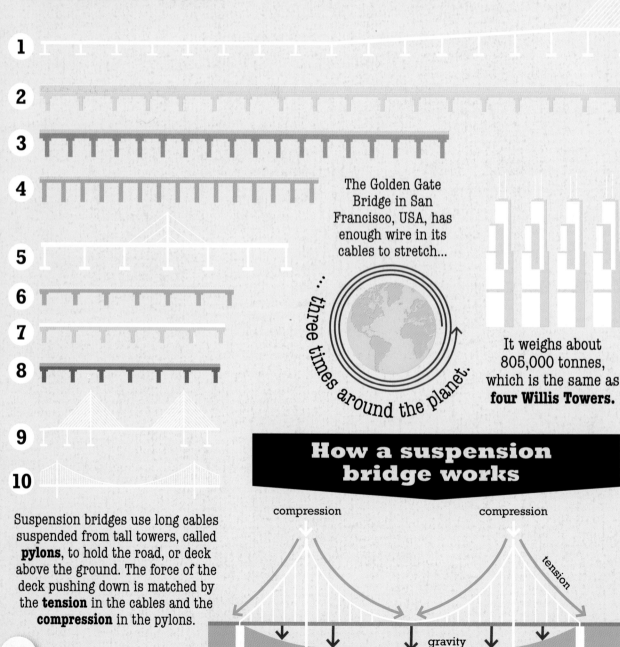

1
2
3
4
5
6
7
8
9
10

The Golden Gate Bridge in San Francisco, USA, has enough wire in its cables to stretch...

...three times around the planet.

It weighs about 805,000 tonnes, which is the same as **four Willis Towers.**

How a suspension bridge works

Suspension bridges use long cables suspended from tall towers, called **pylons**, to hold the road, or deck above the ground. The force of the deck pushing down is matched by the **tension** in the cables and the **compression** in the pylons.

compression

compression

tension

gravity

The Millau Viaduct in France is the tallest bridge in the world, with a height of 343 m – taller than the **Eiffel Tower**.

343 m

The length of the world's longest bridge is greater than the distance between New York City and Philadelphia.

Driving across the world's longest bridge at 60 km/h, it would take a car **about 2 hrs 45 mins to complete the journey.**

LONGEST BRIDGES

1. **Danyang-Kunshan Grand Bridge (China) – 164,800 m**
2. **Tianjin Grand Bridge (China) – 113,700 m**
3. **Weinan Weihe Grand Bridge (China) – 79,732 m**
4. **Bang Na Expressway (Thailand) – 54,000 m**
5. **Beijing Grand Bridge (China) – 48,153 m**
6. **Lake Pontchartrain Causeway (USA) – 38,442 m**
7. **Manchac Swamp Bridge (USA) – 36,710 m**
8. **Yangcun Bridge (China) – 35,812 m**
9. **Hangzhou Bay Bridge (China) - 35,673 m**
10. **Runyang Bridge (China) – 35,660 m**

Widest Bridge

The world's widest bridge is the San Francisco-Oakland Bay Bridge in California, USA. It is **78.7 m** wide, which is more than 10 m wider than the wingspan of a **747-8 Jumbo Jet**.

68.5 m

THAT DOESN'T LOOK RIGHT!

←·····································→

Some buildings are deliberately designed to look different, while others developed problems when they were built. The buildings shown here lean more than any others, some intentionally, while others have faults.

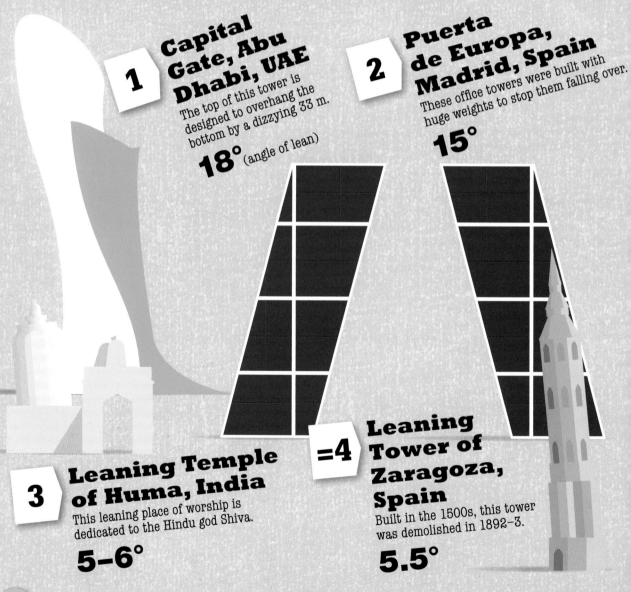

1 **Capital Gate, Abu Dhabi, UAE**
The top of this tower is designed to overhang the bottom by a dizzying 33 m.

18° (angle of lean)

2 **Puerta de Europa, Madrid, Spain**
These office towers were built with huge weights to stop them falling over.

15°

3 **Leaning Temple of Huma, India**
This leaning place of worship is dedicated to the Hindu god Shiva.

5–6°

=4 **Leaning Tower of Zaragoza, Spain**
Built in the 1500s, this tower was demolished in 1892–3.

5.5°

Melting building

sunlight

Nicknamed the 'Walkie-Talkie', the curved shape of this building in the City of London accidentally focusses sunlight on a spot in a nearby street. This creates temperatures of more than 90°C – that's hot enough to melt plastic surfaces on cars and even to fry an egg!

=4 Leaning Tower of Niles, Illinois, USA

Built in 1934, this is a half-sized replica of the Leaning Tower of Pisa.

5.5°

6 Leaning Tower of Suurhusen, Germany

The tower of this church started to lean when wooden beams rotted.

5.19°

7 Leaning Tower of Pisa

Built as a bell tower, this tower leans because it was built on soft ground and without adequate foundations.

3.99°

8 Tower of Garisenda, Bologna, Italy

This is the shorter of two leaning towers in Bologna, but it leans more than the other.

3.8°

=9 Leaning Tower of Nevyansk, Russia

The lean on this tower was caused by the ground beneath subsiding.

3°

=9 Yunyan Pagoda, China

Cracks in supporting pillars have caused this 47-m tower to lean to one side.

3°

Before the Burj Khalifa, the tallest artificial structure was a radio mast built near Warsaw in Poland. It was 646.38 m tall – lying down it would be as long as 45 double-decker buses. It collapsed on 8 August 1991.

SUPERDOMES

Because it has no sharp edges or flat surfaces, a dome is a very strong shape and can be used to cover a huge area. Domes are found on churches, markets and stadiums.

Strong domes

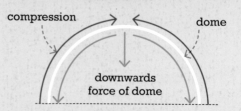

Domes work in the same way as arches. Weight from the top of the dome is distributed down its walls, creating a pressure (or compression) which pushes the dome together, making it even stronger.

St Paul's Cathedral

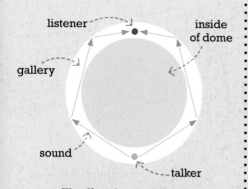

The dome of St Paul's, London, is one of the largest cathedral domes in the world. It weighs about **65,000 tonnes**, which is about the same as a large aircraft carrier.

The first level of the dome is called the Whispering Gallery. The special acoustics mean that a whisper made on one side of the gallery can be heard on the other.

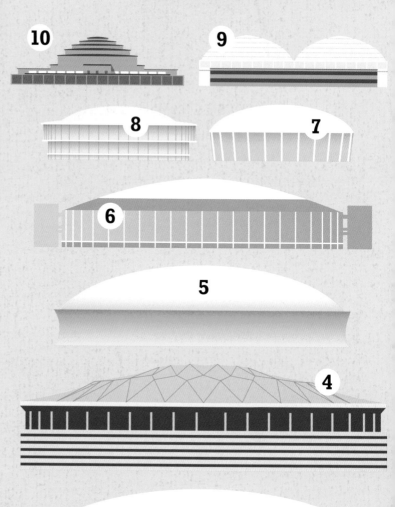

LARGEST DOMES THROUGH HISTORY

1. **New Singapore National Stadium, Singapore (2014–) – 312 m**

2. **Cowboys Stadium, USA (2009–2014) – 275 m**

3. **Oita Stadium, Japan (2001–2009) – 274 m**

4. **Georgia Dome, USA (1992–2001) – 256 m**

5. **Louisiana Superdome, USA (1975–1992) – 207 m**

6. **Astrodome, USA (1965–1975) – 195.5 m**

7. **Belgrade Fair – Hall 1, Serbia (1967–1965) – 109 m**

8. **Bojangles' Coliseum, USA (1955–1957) – 101.5 m**

9. **Leipzig Market Hall, Germany (1930–1955) – 65.5 m**

10. **Centennial Hall, Poland (1913–1930) – 65 m**

2

1

The New Singapore National Stadium is 82.5 m tall, which is about three-fifths the height of the Pyramid of Khufu (see page 19)

Geodesic domes

A geodesic dome combines arches and triangles to create a large, but lightweight covering.

The Fukuoka Yafuoku! Dome, Japan, is one of the largest geodesic domes in the world. This baseball stadium can seat **30,000 people** and it is 84 m tall, almost as tall as the **Statue of Liberty**.

93 m

BUILDING IN SPACE

<‹ ·· ›>

Space stations are designed to support a human crew for many months. They are just like homes in space, with facilities for sleeping, eating, washing and working.

1 **International Space Station (ISS – various)**
The ISS was built jointly by several countries.

907 m³ (volume of pressurised space)

2 **Skylab (USA)**
This orbited Earth from 1973 until it re-entered and burned up in Earth's atmosphere in 1979.

360 m³

3 **Mir (USSR/ Russia)**
This was the first space station that was built in stages and it orbited from 1986 to 2001.

350 m³

=4 **Salyut 5 (USSR)**
This space station was in orbit for just over a year, but was only occupied for 67 days.

100 m³

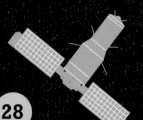

=4 **Salyut 1 (USSR)**
Launched in 1971, this was the first ever space station.

100 m³

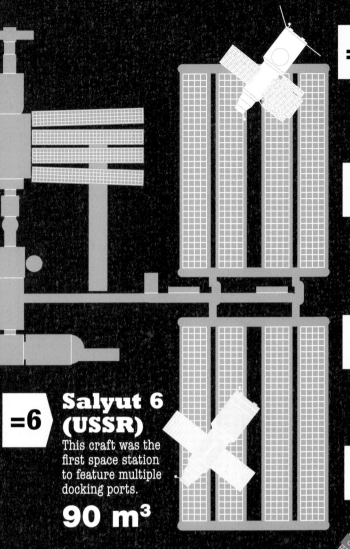

Salyut 7 (USSR)

=6

This was the last station that was part of the Salyut programme and was replaced by Mir.

90 m³

Salyut 4 (USSR)

=6

This space station made more than 12,000 orbits around Earth.

90 m³

Salyut 3 (USSR)

=6

This space station was occupied for just 15 days.

90 m³

Salyut 6 (USSR)

=6

This craft was the first space station to feature multiple docking ports.

90 m³

Tiangong 1 (China)

10

China's first space station. Its name means 'Heavenly Place'.

14.4 m³

ISS facts

The ISS weighs 419.455 tonnes – about the same as two blue whales.

It was built in stages – different modules were launched into space and put together in orbit. The first module, called Zarya, weighed just 19.3 tonnes.

Zarya FGU

The huge solar arrays can produce 110 kw of total power, which is enough to power 55 homes.

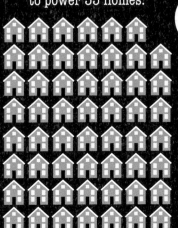

It orbits at a speed of **28,000 km/h,** and it travels around about two-thirds of the planet every hour.

In a single day it travels the equivalent distance from Earth to the Moon and back.

The inside of the International Space Station has the same volume as a Boeing 747 Jumbo Jet – **enough to hold 19 million ping pong balls!** It contains laboratories, an observatory, toilets and washing facilities, and living quarters for the astronauts.

29

GLOSSARY

accelerate
To increase speed.

acoustics
The science of how sound waves behave as they travel through objects. This includes how sound travels through air.

acrylic
A type of plastic that is both lightweight and strong. Acrylic glass is a see-through plastic that is used to make the walls of large aquariums.

aquarium
A glass-walled tank that is designed to hold water and aquatic animals, such as fish, crabs and octopuses. The largest aquariums hold millions of litres of water and hundreds of creatures.

barrow
An ancient burial mound.

blimp
A type of airship without any form of rigid structure inside the envelope (the large sac used to hold the gas that lifts the craft into the air).

deck
In a bridge, this is the surface that carries traffic or pedestrians.

geodesic dome
A type of dome where the walls are made up of triangles.

hectare
A unit used to measure land area. One hectare equals 10,000 sq m.

inflation
When something increases in price.

leasable area
The amount of space in a building that can be leased, or rented, for shops or offices.

mall
A large building that contains lots of shops. Many malls offer other services, such as cinemas, theme parks and restaurants, to keep shoppers entertained.

module
A part or set of parts that can be joined with others to create a larger structure.

pressurised space
In a space station, this is the part of the craft where the atmosphere is under pressure and breathable and where astronauts can survive without wearing a spacesuit.

pylon
A tall vertical structure. In a suspension bridge, the pylons are the tall towers that support the long cables carrying the deck.

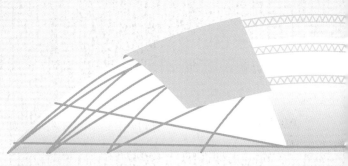

pyramid
A three-dimensional shape with triangular sides. Many civilisations built pyramid-shaped buildings to act as tombs or temples. For example, the ancient Egyptians built the Great Pyramids at Giza more than 4,500 years ago.

relic
The ancient remains of a saint or someone who was considered important.

skyscraper
A tall building that has many floors and is used for offices, hotels and flats.

solar array
The parts of a spacecraft that produce electricity from sunlight.

space station
A type of spacecraft that is designed to orbit Earth and contain everything necessary to support a human crew.

species
A group of organisms that share the same characteristics and are capable of breeding to produce fertile offspring.

suspension bridge
A type of bridge that uses long cables hanging from towers to carry a deck that is suspended above the ground.

suite
A group of rooms. A hotel suite can contain several rooms, including bedrooms, bathrooms, dining areas, a lounge and a games room.

tumulus
A large mound of earth, rock and stones that has been built over a grave. The word is the Latin for 'small hill'.

USSR
Short for the Union of Soviet Socialist Republics, this was the name given to the communist state made up of Russia and its neighbouring countries.

WEBSITES

◄ • ►

MORE INFO:

http://www.emporis.com
A website holding facts, figures, information and images about more than 400,000 important buildings around the world, including the tallest on the planet.

http://www.guinnessworldrecords.com
The website for all things regarding record-breaking. It is packed with thousands of world records and facts.

http://www.nasa.gov/mission_pages/station
The NASA website that contains all the data, images and records about the International Space Station.

MORE GRAPHICS:

www.visualinformation.info
A website that contains a whole host of infographic material on subjects as diverse as natural history, science, sport and computer games.

www.coolinfographics.com
A collection of infographics and data visualisations from other online resources, magazines and newspapers.

www.dailyinfographic.com
A comprehensive collection of infographics on an enormous range of topics that is updated every day!

INDEX

A
airports **20, 21**
Antilia **9**
aquariums **14, 15**

B
bridges **22, 23**
British Museum **10**
Burj al Arab **9**
busiest airports **21**

D-E
domes **26, 27**
Dubai Mall **6**
Dubai Mall Aquarium **15**
Eiffel Tower **4, 23**
Empire State Building **5, 16**

F
fastest roller coasters **12–13**
Ferrari World **13**
Forbidden City **16**
Fukoka Yafuoku! Dome **27**

G-H
geodesic domes **27**
Golden Gate Bridge **22**
Grand Central Terminal **21**
Hengoin Ocean Kingdom **14**
Hotel President Wilson **9**

I-K
International Space Station **28, 29**
Jungle Jim's **7**
King Kullen **7**
KL Bird Park **14**

L
largest aquariums **15**
largest domes **27**
largest royal palaces **17**
largest shopping malls **7**
largest space stations **28–29**
leaning buildings **24, 25**
longest bridges **23**
Louvre **11, 16**

M-N
Marina Bay Sands **8**
Millau Viaduct **23**
most expensive buildings **9**
most popular museums **11**
museums **10, 11**
New Singapore National Stadium **27**

P-R
Palace of Parliament **16, 17**

palaces **16, 17**
ports **20, 21**

S
San Francisco-Oakland Bay Bridge **23**
Shanghai **20, 21**
Sistine Chapel **11**
skyscrapers **4, 5**
Smithsonian Institution **10**
space stations **28, 29**
St Paul's Cathedral **26**
suspension bridges **22**

T-V
theme parks **12, 13**
Toronto Zoo **15**
train stations **20, 21**
Versailles, Palace of **16**

W-Z
Walkie-Talkie building **25**
zoos **15**

Acknowledgements

Published in paperback in 2016
First published in hardback in 2015
Copyright © Wayland 2015

Wayland
Carmelite House
50 Victoria Embankment
London
EC4Y 0DZ

All rights reserved.

10 9 8 7 6 5 4 3 2 1

www.hachette.co.uk

Series editor: Julia Adams

Produced by Tall Tree Ltd
Editor: Jon Richards
Designer: Ed Simkins

Dewey classification: 720-dc23

ISBN: 9780750297837
Library ebook ISBN: 9780750287487

Printed in Malaysia
Wayland is a division of Hachette
Children's Group, an Hachette UK
company.

The website addresses (URL
included in this book were u
at the time of going to press
However, because of the na
of the Internet, it is possible
some addresses may have
changed, or sites may have
changed or closed down, si
publication. While the autho
and Publisher regret any
inconvenience this may cau
the readers, no responsibilit
for any such changes can be
accepted by either the auth
or the Publisher.